TIME TO COMPARE!

Which IS TALLER?

T0009857

BY JAGGER YOUSSEF

Gareth Stevens
PUBLISHING

first concepts

We can compare!
The girl is taller.

3

The man is taller.

5

The purple flower
is taller.

7

The red candle
is taller.

8

9

The brown horse
is taller.

The blue house
is taller.

13

The white chair
is taller.

14

15

The green tree
is taller.

17

The pink cup is taller.

19

The yellow slide
is taller.

21

Point to the
taller animal.

23

Please visit our website, www.garethstevens.com. For a free color catalog of all our high-quality books, call toll free 1-800-542-2595 or fax 1-877-542-2596.

Library of Congress Cataloging-in-Publication Data
Names: Youssef, Jagger, author.
Title: Which is taller? / Jagger Youssef.
Description: New York : Gareth Stevens Publishing, [2021] | Series: Time to compare! | Includes index.
Identifiers: LCCN 2019042303 | ISBN 9781538255001 (library binding) | ISBN 9781538254981 (paperback) | ISBN 9781538254998 (6 Pack) | ISBN 9781538255018 (ebook)
Subjects: LCSH: Measurement–Juvenile literature. | Size judgment–Juvenile literature. | Comparison (Psychology) in children–Juvenile literature.
Classification: LCC QC90.6 .Y68 2021 | DDC 530.8–dc23
LC record available at https://lccn.loc.gov/2019042303

First Edition

Published in 2021 by
Gareth Stevens Publishing
111 East 14th Street, Suite 349
New York, NY 10003

Copyright © 2021 Gareth Stevens Publishing

Designer: Sarah Liddell
Editor: Therese Shea

Photo credits: Cover, p. 1 (main) Jan Martin Will/Shutterstock.com; cover, p. 1 (background) oksanka007/Shutterstock.com; p. 3 Tatyana Vyc/Shutterstock.com; p. 5 (woman) szefei/Shutterstock.com; p. 5 (man) Aaron Amat/Shutterstock.com; p. 7 (pink flower) Kisialiou Yury/Shutterstock.com; p. 7 (purple flower) Lopatin Anton/Shutterstock.com; p. 9 (red candle) 1000isolate/Shutterstock.com; p. 9 (orange candle) Nutink/Shutterstock.com; p. 11 (brown horse) Four Oaks/Shutterstock.com; pp. 11 (black horse), 23 (lion) Eric Isselee/Shutterstock.com; p. 13 (brown house) Robynrg/Shutterstock.com; p. 13 (blue house) Nadya Kubik/Shutterstock.com; p. 15 SOMPOPSRINOPHAN/Shutterstock.com; p. 17 (green tree) Sanit Fuangnakhon/Shutterstock.com; p. 17 (red tree) 24Novembers/Shutterstock.com; p. 19 (pink cup) Pandan Alas/Shutterstock.com; p. 19 (green cup) Studio KIWI/Shutterstock.com; p. 21 (red slide) happymay/Shutterstock.com; p. 21 (yellow slide) SabOlga/Shutterstock.com; p. 23 (giraffe) g_tech/Shutterstock.com.

Printed in the United States of America

Some of the images in this book illustrate individuals who are models. The depictions do not imply actual situations or events.

CPSIA compliance information: Batch #CS20GS: For further information contact Gareth Stevens, New York, New York at 1-800-542-2595.

Find us on